SUPERSTARS OF WRESTLING

KENNY OMEGA

BY BENJAMIN PROUDFIT

Gareth Stevens
PUBLISHING

HOT TOPICS

Please visit our website, www.garethstevens.com. For a free color catalog of all our high-quality books, call toll free 1-800-542-2595 or fax 1-877-542-2596.

Library of Congress Cataloging-in-Publication Data

Names: Proudfit, Benjamin, author.
Title: Kenny Omega / Benjamin Proudfit.
Description: New York : Gareth Stevens Publishing, 2022. | Series: Superstars of wrestling | Includes index.
Identifiers: LCCN 2020032249 (print) | LCCN 2020032250 (ebook) | ISBN 9781538265918 (library binding) | ISBN 9781538265895 (paperback) | ISBN 9781538265901 (set) | ISBN 9781538265925 (ebook)
Subjects: LCSH: Omega, Kenny, 1983- --Juvenile literature. | World Wrestling Entertainment, Inc.--Biography--Juvenile literature. | Wrestlers--Japan--Biography--Juvenile literature.
Classification: LCC GV1196.O64 P76 2022 (print) | LCC GV1196.O64 (ebook) | DDC 796.812092 [B]--dc23
LC record available at https://lccn.loc.gov/2020032249
LC ebook record available at https://lccn.loc.gov/2020032250

First Edition

Published in 2022 by
Gareth Stevens Publishing
111 East 14th Street, Suite 349
New York, NY 10003

Copyright © 2022 Gareth Stevens Publishing

Designer: Michael Flynn
Editor: Kristen Nelson

Photo credits: Cover, pp. 1, 15, 17, 19, 29 New Japan Pro-Wrestling//Getty Images; pp. 5, 7, 11 Etsuo Hara/Getty Images; p. 9 Masashi Hara/Getty Images; p. 13 https://commons.wikimedia.org/wiki/Category:Bullet_Club#/media/File:Kenny_Omega_2016.jpg; p. 21 https://commons.wikimedia.org/wiki/Category:Kenny_Omega#/media/File:The_ELITE_(professional_wrestling).jpg; pp. 23, 25 Emma McIntyre/Getty Images; p. 27 Mike Coppola/Getty Images.

All rights reserved. No part of this book may be reproduced in any form without permission in writing from the publisher, except by a reviewer.

Printed in the United States of America

CPSIA compliance information: Batch #CSGS22: For further information contact Gareth Stevens, New York, New York at 1-800-542-2595.

CONTENTS

Meet Kenny Omega	4
Early Start	6
A Golden Team	10
G1 Winner	14
Facing Okada	16
Going All In	20
Elite in AEW	22
Tag Team Champs	26
Kenny's Future	28
The Best of Kenny Omega	30
For More Information	31
Glossary	32
Index	32

MEET KENNY OMEGA

Kenny Omega is one of the best **professional** wrestlers in the world today. But, he's not the best known! Kenny, born Tyson Smith on October 16, 1983, has wrestled all over the world. Today, he performs with All **Elite** Wrestling (AEW).

IN THE RING

Kenny is from Winnipeg, Manitoba, in Canada.

EARLY START

Kenny had his first **match** when he was a teenager. Even then, those who saw it knew he'd be a star. Kenny trained in Deep South Wrestling, a **developmental** part of World Wrestling Entertainment (WWE). But, in 2006, he walked away.

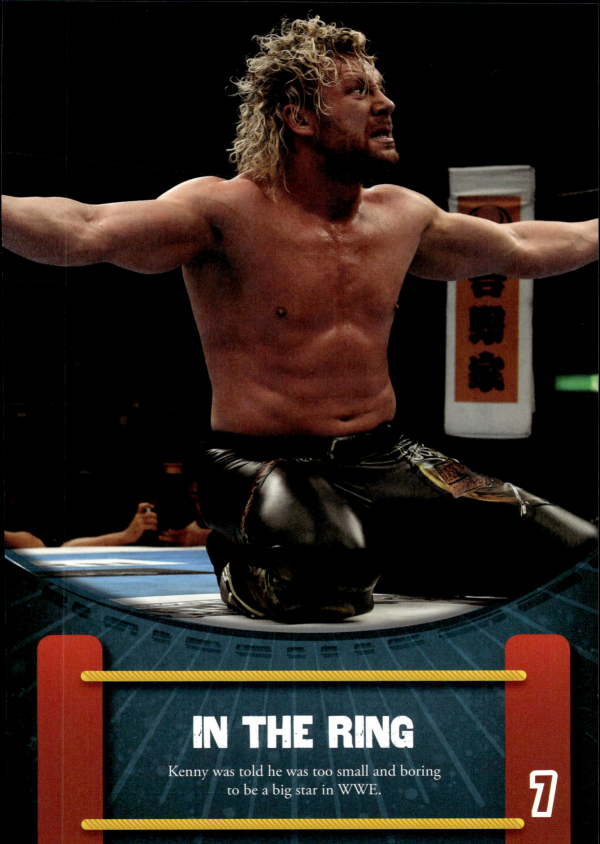

IN THE RING

Kenny was told he was too small and boring to be a big star in WWE.

7

Kenny began to follow his own path. That led him to DDT Pro-Wrestling, a top **independent** wrestling company in Japan. Over the next few years, he wrestled around the world, including with New Japan Pro-Wrestling (NJPW) and Ring of Honor.

IN THE RING

Kenny partly chose DDT in order to work with Japanese wrestlers like Kota Ibushi. The two became close friends.

A GOLDEN TEAM

Kenny and Ibushi became a tag team in 2009. They went on to win the IWGP Jr. Heavyweight Tag Team Championship in NJPW together and became beloved by fans. At times, they fought each other in matches full of dangerous, high-flying moves too.

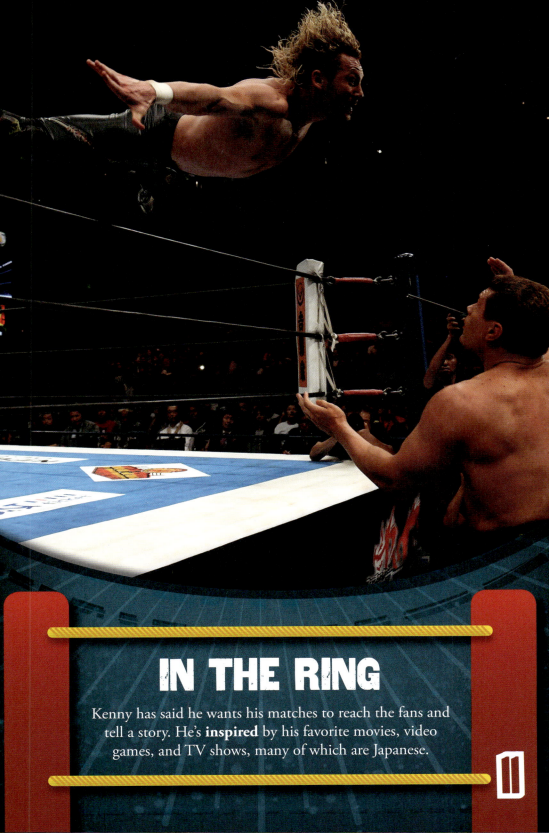

IN THE RING

Kenny has said he wants his matches to reach the fans and tell a story. He's **inspired** by his favorite movies, video games, and TV shows, many of which are Japanese.

Kenny and Ibushi's tag team continued until Kenny joined the Bullet Club in 2014. Two years later, Kenny became the leader of the NJPW group. He also had worked hard and moved from the junior heavyweights to the heavyweights.

IN THE RING

Other past members of the Bullet Club include A.J. Styles, Prince Devitt (known in the WWE as Finn Bálor), Cody, and tag team the Young Bucks.

13

G1 WINNER

In 2016, Kenny made history. He became the first non-Japanese wrestler to win the G1 Climax, NJPW's yearly **tournament**. He had also held the IWGP Intercontinental Championship that year. He was becoming one of global wrestling's biggest stars.

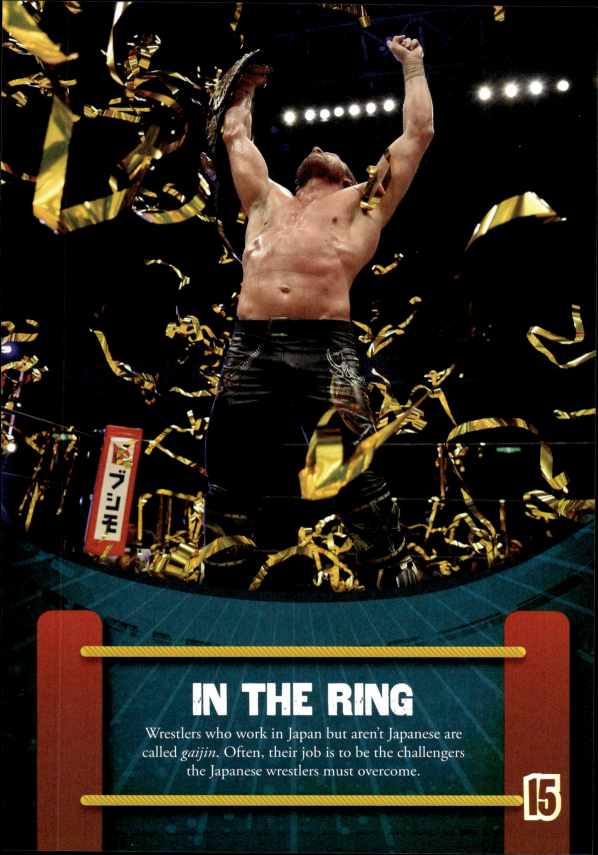

IN THE RING

Wrestlers who work in Japan but aren't Japanese are called *gaijin*. Often, their job is to be the challengers the Japanese wrestlers must overcome.

15

FACING OKADA

The year 2016 also began Kenny's greatest series of matches yet. At Wrestle Kingdom 11, he faced Kazuchika Okada for the IWGP Heavyweight Championship, the top honor in NJPW. Kenny lost, but some call it the greatest pro wrestling match of all time!

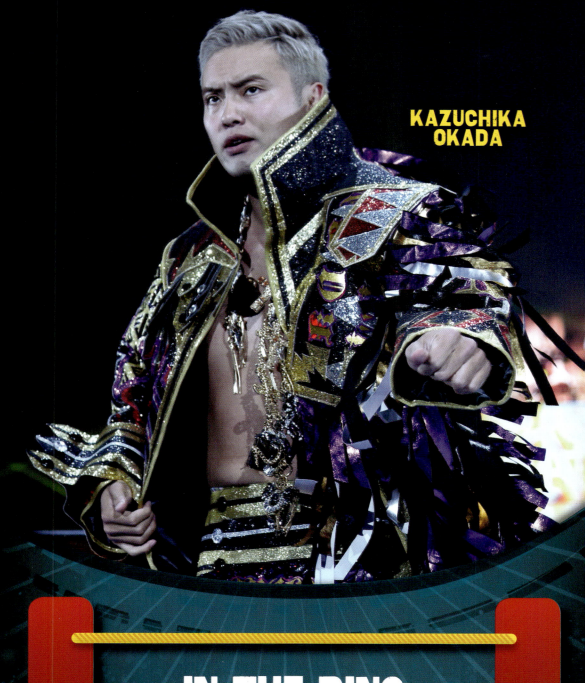

KAZUCHIKA OKADA

IN THE RING

Wrestle Kingdom is NJPW's largest show of the year held in the huge Tokyo Dome every January.

17

Kenny and Okada faced off twice in 2017. The first match ended in a **draw**. Kenny won the second, but the title wasn't on the line. Then, in June 2018 at NJPW Dominion, Kenny and Okada fought for the IWGP Heavyweight Championship again. Kenny won!

IN THE RING

Kenny lost the championship to Hiroshi Tanahashi at Wrestle Kingdom 13.

GOING ALL IN

Kenny wants to make the pro wrestling business better. In September 2018, he was part of the biggest independent wrestling show in many years, called All In. Kenny took on Pentagon, winning a match many said was the best of the night.

IN THE RING

Kenny and the Young Bucks started The Elite in 2016. Their YouTube channel, Being the Elite, also features Cody Rhodes and Adam Page. Cody and the Young Bucks planned All In.

21

ELITE IN AEW

Kenny left NJPW in 2019. He had become such a big star, he could have joined any company around the world. Kenny chose to sign a five-year deal with a new company started by Cody and the Young Bucks: All Elite Wrestling (AEW).

IN THE RING
Kenny serves as an executive vice president of AEW.

23

Kenny felt AEW fit his ideas about wrestling: "I'm trying to open up the world to what wrestling can be and show there is no limitation to what wrestling can be." Kenny's first AEW matches were as part of a tag team with Adam Page.

TAG TEAM CHAMPS

Kenny and Adam Page won the AEW Tag Team Championship in January 2020. They beat tag team SCU to become the second tag team champs in AEW ever. Kenny and Adam held on to the title in a match against the Young Bucks in February.

IN THE RING

In August 2019, Kenny wrestled with Lucha Libre AAA in Mexico. He won the AAA Mega Championship and held the title into 2020.

KENNY'S FUTURE

He hits big moves from the top rope and helps lesser known wrestlers succeed. There's no question that Kenny Omega is one of the best in the ring today. What more could he do in the future?

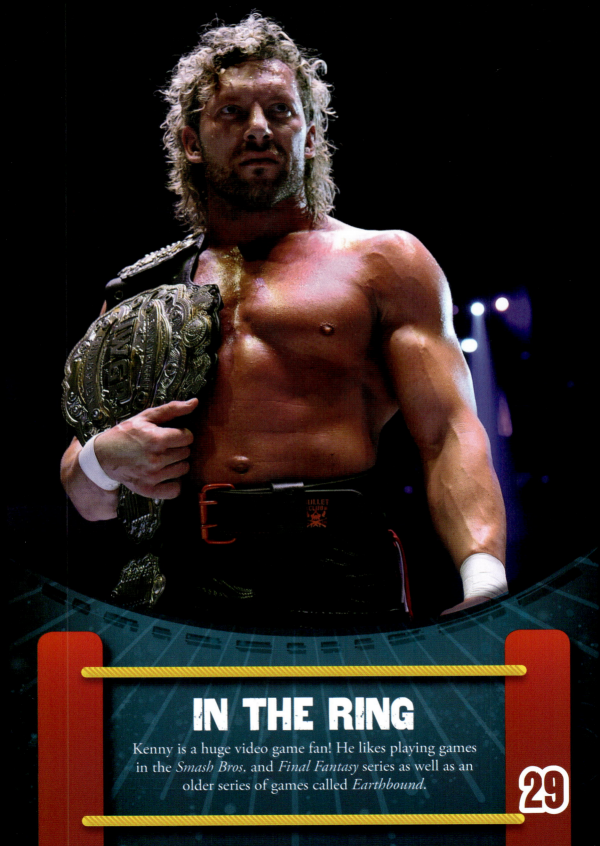

IN THE RING

Kenny is a huge video game fan! He likes playing games in the *Smash Bros.* and *Final Fantasy* series as well as an older series of games called *Earthbound*.

29

THE BEST OF KENNY OMEGA

SIGNATURE MOVES
450 splash, v-trigger

FINISHERS
one-winged angel

ACCOMPLISHMENTS
IWGP Junior Heavyweight Tag Team Champion, IWGP Heavyweight Champion, AEW Tag Team Champion

MATCHES TO WATCH
Wrestle Kingdom 11 vs. Okada; Dominion 2018 vs. Okada; All In 2018 vs. Pentagon

FOR MORE INFORMATION

BOOKS

Borth, Teddy. *A.J. Styles: The Phenomenal One*. Minneapolis, MN: Abdo Zoom, 2018.

Scheff, Matt. *Pro Wrestling's Greatest Matches*. Minneapolis, MN: Sportszone, an imprint of Abdo Publishing, 2017.

WEBSITES

All Elite Wrestling
www.allelitewrestling.com/roster
Follow Kenny Omega and the other wrestlers in AEW here.

Kenny Omega
prowrestling.fandom.com/wiki/Kenny_Omega
Check out more about Kenny Omega's history as a wrestler on this fan-updated page.

Publisher's note to educators and parents: Our editors have carefully reviewed these websites to ensure that they are suitable for students. Many websites change frequently, however, and we cannot guarantee that a site's future contents will continue to meet our high standards of quality and educational value. Be advised that students should be closely supervised whenever they access the internet.

GLOSSARY

developmental: having to do with the growth of something or someone
draw: the end of a game or contest that doesn't have a winner
elite: having to do with having success or power
independent: not owned by a larger business
inspire: to give someone an idea of what to create
match: a contest between two or more people
professional: earning money from an activity that many people do for fun
tournament: a sports contest that many teams or people take part in over the course of many days

INDEX

All Elite Wrestling (AEW) 4, 22, 23, 24, 26
All In 20, 21
Bullet Club, the 12, 13
championships 10, 14, 16, 18, 26, 27
DDT Pro-Wrestling 8
Deep South Wrestling 6
G1 Climax 14
Ibushi, Kota 8, 9, 10, 12
New Japan Pro-Wrestling (NJPW) 8, 10, 12, 14, 16, 17, 18, 22
Okada, Kazuchika 16, 17, 18
Page, Adam 21, 24, 26, 27
Ring of Honor 8
World Wrestling Entertainment (WWE) 6, 7, 13
Wrestle Kingdom 16, 17, 18
Young Bucks, the 13, 21, 22, 26